Dragonfly Dance

Shedding Skins: Four Sioux Poets
Edited by Adrian C. Louis | 978-0-87013-823-2

Writing Home: Indigenous Narratives of Resistance
Michael D. Wilson | 978-0-87013-818-8

National Monuments
Heid E. Erdrich | 978-0-87013-848-5

The Indian Who Bombed Berlin and Other Stories
Ralph Salisbury | 978-0-87013-847-8

Facing the Future: The Indian Child Welfare Act at 30
Edited by Matthew L. M. Fletcher, Wenona T. Singel,
and Kathryn E. Fort | 978-0-87013-860-7

Dragonfly Dance
Denise K. Lajimodiere | 978-0-87013-982-6

Dragonfly Dance

POEMS BY *Denise K. Lajimodiere*

MICHIGAN STATE UNIVERSITY PRESS ▪ *East Lansing*

♾ The paper used in this publication meets the minimum requirements
of ANSI/NISO Z39.48-1992 (R 1997) (Permanence of Paper).

 Michigan State University Press
East Lansing, Michigan 48823-5245

Printed and bound in the United States of America.

16 15 14 13 12 11 10   1 2 3 4 5 6 7 8 9 10

LIBRARY OF CONGRESS CATALOGING-IN-PUBLICATION DATA
Lajimodiere, Denise K.
Dragonfly dance / Denise K. Lajimodiere.
p. cm.
ISBN 978-0-87013-982-6 (pbk. : alk. paper)
I. Title.
PS3612.A48D73 2010
811.'6—dc22
2010003511

Cover design by David Drummond, Salamander Hill Design
Book design by Charlie Sharp, Sharp Des!gns, Lansing, Mich.

green
press
INITIATIVE Michigan State University Press is a member of the Green
Press Initiative and is committed to developing and
encouraging ecologically responsible publishing practices. For more
information about the Green Press Initiative and the use of recycled
paper in book publishing, please visit www.greenpressinitiative.org.

Visit Michigan State University Press on the World Wide Web at
www.msupress.msu.edu

For Leola

To Kianah Giizh Ikwe, Nipinugezik,
MaanaEsha, and Brystin

Even though dragonflies abound, most people tend not to notice them simply because they are not paying attention.

—Forrest L. Mitchell & James L. Lasswell, *A Dazzle of Dragonflies*

CONTENTS

Acknowledgments

Chi miigwech to Louise Erdrich, Heid Erdrich, and the Turtle Mountain Writers Workshop. Your wisdom and encouragement helped me find my voice and galvanized me into completing this manuscript; Dr. Larry Wowoide, Poet Laureate of North Dakota and mentor. Lise Erdrich for constant faith in me. Angie Erdrich-Patel for long Dakota winters filled with the warmth of your friendship and wild rice soup. Loretta DeLong, for your unwavering friendship and remarkable wisdom. Judy Kakenawash Azure for Ojibwe traditions and coffee on the deck. Les LaFountain's loft. Gordon and Cheryl Belcourt, friends, mentors. My daughter Josette 'LaQuette,' and son Loring Riel 'Sky Boy.' Thank you to the Vermont Studio Center where much of this manuscript was finalized. *Miigwech* to Marilyn Nelson and her Soul Mountain retreat. *Chi miigwech* to the beautiful Turtle Mountain people, Métis, and Chippewa, who sit at the heart of this Turtle Island, a sacred and spiritual place, a healing place I call home.

INTRODUCTION

If healing is partly the resurrection and acknowledgement of pain, then Denise Lajimodiere is a healer through her poetry. If healing is partly laughter, then Denise's poetry can laugh through tears. If healing is a mysterious process, Denise shows that it also begins in everyday kindness.

The poems in *Dragonfly Dance* are raw, funny, honest, and also acutely sensitive to a child's point of view. A little girl ignores her brown skinned Barbie and tells her mother she wants to grow up white. We feel the bewilderment and terror of a child praying for her drunken father NOT to make it home, and later, the visceral sorrow of a woman at her father's deathbed, unable to mourn him. The poem "Drunkard's Mass" is both hilarious and sad. The hypocrisy and insult of the Catholic Church's treatment of Native children is woven through the entire book and contrasts with the difficult gathering of wisdom. The trajectory of the book brings us to the healing of ancient traumas through dance, through vision, and especially through the kindness of elders and spiritual connections with animals associated with the Turtle Mountains.

The poems are fierce in their personal invocation of history. A Turtle Mountain grandmother presses her wrist to a starving infant's lips to try and save its life during the winter of 1888. That was the time shortly after the reservation was reduced from 20 townships in North Dakota to only 2 townships. There were no animals to hunt on a range so tiny. There were no crops. The United States government forgot to send the supplies it had promised. There was mass starvation on the reservation in those years, while on the land surrounding, homesteaded by white settlers, cattle fattened and were sold.

The terrible truths of history still live on in the generations since, and Denise's poems are about the working out of history through the heart.

The dragonfly is a lightness of spirit, warrior spirit, water spirit. The dragonfly was sacred to Crazy Horse, and he painted it on his shield as his protector. In the final section of the book, Denise writes of her own connection "we dance, we dance, we dance / to wipe away the tears." She also explores the connection between dancers and the spirit of the dragonfly. One friend tells of surviving a car accident, and of dragonflies gathering around her. A brother says, "they are our ancestors healing you."

I first knew Denise Lajimodiere as a traditional jingle dress dancer. The jingle dress dance was revealed to an Ojibwe elder in a dream—his granddaughter was terribly ill, and he saw in a dream that she would be healed by women from each direction dancing through the sky. In his dream, the sky women wore dresses with small cones of silver that made music in time with their steps. At any powwow today, these beautiful dresses and their dances embody the vision of that dream. The jingle dance is exciting, moving, and quietly comforting. When the music of the dresses rings through the air the vibrations set up a sense of well being and of hope in everyone in the circle of their remarkable sound.

All of her life these poems have been danced out by Denise, and only now that she has the time to reflect and feel has she allowed them to move through her dancing into this writing.

This is a book of pain and power that also makes you laugh out loud. If you listen to the dancing as you read, don't be surprised if you are also healed.

LOUISE ERDRICH, 2010

Out Steppin'

Out Steppin'

I ask my mom where she's going.
Out steppin' she says, a black patent
leather purse draped over her arm.
She outlines her lips in red
without a mirror, drops the case
into her bag, and closes the tortoiseshell
latch with a snap that tells him
let's go.

I wrap my arms around a leg
and beg her not to leave
us, my sister and I wail
and slap the door as it slams shut.
Our brother grabs us by our braids
and drags us down the hall,
ties the mamma cat up in a paper
bag and throws her down the stairs,
over and over we scream. He rips the head
off our favorite doll, then pins
me down first, lays heaving
on top, brown, stinking hand
over my mouth. Later he strangles
a kitten in front of us and says he'll kill
the rest if we tell.

In the morning tiny, pink, plastic babies
in our shoes, a race car in his.

The Necklace

Once a mouse nosed
    its way into my dresser drawer
        and chewed through a beaded
    necklace, getting to the penny candy
beneath, rainbow colored coconut candy,

my favorite.
    My mom had made the beaded loom necklace,
        her arthritic fingers patiently
    threading beads
on the long thin needle, weaving,

night after night.
    She bent to repairing the necklace,
        and I pleaded to wear it to school.
    At recess a White boy
ran by, yanked

it off my neck, and threw it.
    I watched as it ascended
        high above the blacktop;
    the beads glittered, scattering their light,
a rainbow against gray skies.

Bag Balm

All hail the chartreuse can of lanolin
good for all tits whether attached to
the four legged or the two.
Good for itches, bad for the cavalry

who killed all my grandmother's cows
chickens and pigs on their way
to find Little Shell, they never found
the chipped china hidden

in the well, or the berry money,
wrapped in plastic, safe
in square Bag Balm cans
buried under the birch wood pile.

The Quilt

Twenty five cents'll buy a bundle of white
people's leftover clothes from the church,
wrapped in a skirt and tied tight,

a Latin missal folded inside.
Grandma's been known to knock
her calico dressed, braided sisters

plumb sideways if they tried reaching
for the bundle she had her eye on.
By kerosene lamp and wood stove fire,

I'd sit with her steadying a seam,
the *brrrup* of her razor
cutting through the threads;

zippers laid in El Roi-Tan cigar
boxes, buttons rattling in a Bag Balm can.
Squares cut from wool

skirts, and coats pieced together,
six stitches to the inch,
she said, a lesson learned the hard

way from boarding school nuns.
An army blanket as batting,
a length of calico for backing,

stitched together with yarn unraveled
from a worn red sweater,
unraveled like the treaty,

less than a quarter an acre bought
this reservation they bundled us onto,
ishkoonigan, leftover land.

Indian Angel in 1st Grade

Sister Kathryn from Indiana
I know you don't approve of me,
a half-breed child
from the bush, log cabin, dirt floor.
With ruler in hand you say with a sniff
I can tell a lot by a child's fingernails,
and have us hold out our tiny trembling hands.
My darned socks don't match.
My charity soles have holes.
My hair is *shaykaweesh*.
I smell of smoke and muskrat tails,
and my nails aren't clean.
I can't seem to stop
myself from becoming
small enough to fit on
a pinhead
but here I
sit.
Sister, how many angels fit
on the head of a pin?

Sweat Lodge

1.

We hear you crying.
Pray with sweet grass,
the smoke carries your prayers to the
Creator;
we will help you,
Woman of the North.

2.

Sitting Bull's young wife
came in one evening,
you think you are so
pretty with your ways
with the warriors,
in my day
you should have seen me.

3.

You must find your way as
an Anishinaabe, woman from the North,
you are not Lakota;
we send you on
your journey home.

St. Ignatius

Come back to the Sanctuary
with me girls,
said the augur of pagan Rome
pulling quarters
from behind ears
and eggs from his cassock.

Parochial prurient priest
working magic tricks
with doughy hands.

Feeling our chests
to make sure bras weren't
worn those Saturday
Catechism mornings.

They are not good for you.
Yes father, no father
no bras.
Jesus loves good Catholic girls.

The Bundles of St. Ann's

Josephte shit her pants while she held
    the door but refused to give up her spot.
      Cleophe fell down the stairs
        shouting to the nun

which bundle she wanted
    before being hauled
      off to the Indian Health Service Hospital
        and treated for a broken ankle.

Appoline grabbed
    a man's shoe that Alvina held the match
      to and wouldn't give it up.
        Alvina bought the one shoe

for 25¢, pleased, smiling
    at her husband looking at
      the shoe set before him
        on the kitchen table.

The Reservation Dump

We drank from plastic bottles,
tossed them into plastic bags,
carried them to garbage cans,
picked up by tribal workers
and taken to the reservation dump
where gleaming BIA front-end loaders
shuddered as they buried it
then smoothed the rich black dirt
over the wounds to cover generations
of stink and putrid rot.
Later, tribal elected officials and HUD
build hundred-thousand-dollar
homes on top, name it Prairie View
and move in the Indians.
Cancer rates go sky high, and IHS doctors
conduct research studies as
babies die while thick black mold
creeps up bedroom walls.
Housing officials peering under foundation
spaces find nothing amiss, only a rusted
car body crawling out of the earth,
empty sockets like a vulture's skull.

Warm Morning at Ft. Totten

The single pane windows rattle like a Gatling gun,
        the punishing Dakota plains winter relentless.

The little boys march to the bathroom
        down two flights of wood stairs, through a long narrow

hallway, dark.
        The cement troughs sit low,

two boys to a trough,
        a seashell shaped depression for the rough soap,

each boy has his own spigot of cold water.
        They are marched back to their dorm,

marched by the cast iron wood stove, stamped *Warm Morning*,
        shivering,

hungry, bone tired from work in the barn, in the fields,
        in the harness shop, marching, always marching.

The stove stands sentinel at the head of the room,
        listening to the snaps of springs, as tiny limbs seek warmth.

My Grandfather Was a New Initiate

My grandfather was a new initiate
at the Ft. Totten Indian boarding school.
He was told he had to steal a can of tomatoes,
a sweet fruit to these hungry little boys in the dorm.

Down the cement stairs,
past the headmaster's studio
with its own bath,
into the Dakota dark
he stumbled across Cavalry Square
to the outside kitchen shed door,
fumbled for the hanging string,
down the narrow stairs,
grabbed the heavy can and lit
out into the steel arm of the headmaster.

They brought me to the magazine room
where a barrel was strung across.
I had to lay over it, and two bigger boys held my arms.
The little boys had to watch.
The headmaster whipped my bare back with a rubber hose.
Uh, uh! I couldn't breathe,
couldn't catch my breath.
I passed out.
The boys said they had to hold me up for one more whip.

At Ft. Totten today
red bricks crumble
beneath white paint.
Name plaques on the buildings
recognize its days as a fort
and then a boarding school.

Standing inside the black powder/flour storage room,
it's small,
maybe ten by ten.
How did all the little boys fit?

As I stood and wept,
the hot July winds
gathered forces from across the plains
and hurled like warriors
into the square,
an arrow soaked in gunpowder,
lit, aimed and the room exploded around
me, the bricks a liquid red.

The Moccasin Trail

I will not take the trail of cowboy boots,
or spike heels and pointed pumps.
My path is far less traveled.

I will softly walk the moccasin trail,
through the galaxies of star spirits
to the place where my ancestors
have gone, the path of ancient souls.
The guardian bear will ask my spirit name;
I will call out a name forever meant for his ears only.
In new white moccasins, with sparkling beaded soles
on my feet, I'll take my place among the stars.

Ogichida Ikwewag

Red Lake 5.20.05

The elders sent out a call
gathering us from the four directions.
It was time for the medicine dress dancers
to dance, to wipe away the tears.

A hundred strong, ogichida ikwewag,
gathered beneath the watchful moon,
stepping into the cedar circle,
our jingles silver tears,

joining the children's spirits,
dancing around the drum's
healing beat, our hearts
one in prayer.

Ziibaaska'iganagooday
sang across Aki,
our eagle fans swept the air,
sending prayers to Manitou,

carried on spirit wings.
And from the cobalt sky above,
Nookomis nodded and wrapped us
in her blanket of light.

Obodashkwanishi

The grandkids on the low bridge over the coulee
waved frantically for me to hurry.
Launching themselves straight up
from the water
the dragonflies a whirlwind of joy.
We stood and watched
feeling like we had balcony
seats at an aerial show.

Today I saw the dragonfly
Come from the wells where he did lie.

Their wings made a delicate electric buzz
as they wheeled about each other.

Thro' crofts and pastures wet with dew
A living flash of light he flew.

The rising happiness,
I felt a power
flow into me like a river,
watching these holy creatures.

ALFRED TENNYSON, "The Two Voices, 1883"

Dragonfly Dance

Suspended above our plumed
and feathered heads

the dragonflies join
us for Grand Entry at Red Lake,

the sun striking flames
from their sapphire wings,

these winged mounts
of ancestor spirits,

returning to heal.
I move in step with the drum;

I dance with the dragonflies
As one drops down

to gaze into my face
with its lovely bright eyes.

I hold its gaze, this holy creature,
spirit of the water,

born of the water as I am,
life, birth, power of love made constant.

She spins her beaded body
to join the dragonfly dance,

as my wings join their rhythm,
my feet vibrating.

Midnight in North Dakota

Eagle plumes,
beaded on night's velour
glitter in frozen air,
floating on heads of shadowy forms.

In the northern sky, spirits spiral and soar,
cascading over turtle hills.
As the dazzling curtains rise and fall
we stand beneath the elegance
of our ancestors' healing dance.
The downy comfort of fallen snow
smoothly covering the sleeping turtles.

It's storytelling time.

To My Sister

We slept together,
our dreams tangled like
our long black hair.
On rainy nights
we held hands and jumped off
the narrow cot so *kookoosh*
wouldn't grab our ankles
on the dark way to the bathroom.
Hand in hand we'd walk to St. Peter's school,
our wool uniforms itching,
eyes smarting from grandma's tight
braids, stomachs warm
from bannock soaked in bacon grease.
We'd spend our ten cents at the Goodwill,
milk shake at the corner Five and Dime
looking so alike we passed for twins;
he couldn't tell us apart or didn't bother to,
sometimes, after his smelly hands and breath
we had to dance ourselves back to life.

I'm tired,
let's jump
to the other side.

Automatic Starter

Be my car starter
in the coming bitter blue winter,

leave my flannelled bed
and step into the blueblack night

of 6 A.M. The glittered snow
a Styrofoam crunch beneath

leather boots, to unplug
the heater cord.

I don't need a man to blanket
me with jealousy

to wrap me in possessiveness
to be my self confidence.

Be my car starter
in windchills of thirty below,

so I can dash through the stiff air
and climb into the yawing heat

of the cab, softened, warm,
like the down comforted bed

I just left. Alone.

The Warrior

We don't speak of love, the Indian and the babe,
taboo this feeling; can't talk about it,
only in ceremony.

During a Lenten nightmare, the *rugaroo*
danced backwards with the Ace of Spades
to his forehead the night I confessed my love.

A warrior in passionate battle charge,
bagamaagan raised,
the northern plains bureaucrat,
the southwest desert urban Indian,
shouting buffalo calls to the moon.

Boise Forte Man

Beware the man
who says, *Listen to this*
song and you will know me.
A country western strain
of sorrowful sobbing drunken
squeaks and yowels
and slobberly lips
as he pumps poison into
your hips
and tubes glow
red hot in the night
as the radio hisses.
And tubes twist,
damages as he explodes.
You done me wrong.
Listen to me
and know my song.

B.J.

Your breath smelled of Lummi
and Jack Daniels.
Your black, bowl-cut hair held up your
twisted face and grimaced lips, so close to mine
the razor knife to my neck.
An army AWOL warrior.
If I can't have you, nobody will;
they'll find your body in the forest;
you'll be front page news
tomorrow morning.

Through your eight-year-old eyes
the house with your mother in it burned again.
Totem poles fell and potlatches were abandoned;
drums were stilled, canoes beached,
and whales mourned.
The forest yearns for you to
climb a cedar tree
and watch the last of the evening's sunset.

Northern Lights

The Chippewa say
      the Northern Lights
are spirits dancing
      their connection
with us here on earth,

    reaching,
        arching,
           joyous

at the end of the long moccasin trail.

Don't whistle at them!

    or they will
      come down
        and choke you.

You, a spirit
    as big as the wind
painting the Northern Lights
    with Red Star Constellation
Buffalo spirits.

And Indian heaven
    is a man wearing a soft,
      worn painter's shirt.

Night Owls

In memory of Don Rush

When the aching sets
in and my soul is crying,
when night owls fly
around inside my head,
you tell stories
until I fall
asleep.

Sonnet

Pablo kept his many women poor
In love and money, confused, I ask you why.
You look at me and laugh and nearly roar,
Because he's Picasso! flinging arms up high.
Diego likened sex to taking a piss.
The hands caressing nudes betrayed his wife;
Then he took her sister, adding emphasis
To her pain; always under the knife,
And through her painted layers Frida moans.
An artist rich in fame, I call you Pablo
Diego; won't speak of love in English tones.
Although I see your kiss means only woe,
As you reach for me, and on your bed I fall,
I glimpse the painted nudes up on your wall.

Oven Bread

He only gives hugs on demand,
doesn't say I love you,
but loves warm days
and Feather, his dog;
calls me babe,
serves Starbucks in bed
with oven bread;
evening dinners out,
a warm bathrobe
after a cool shower;
holds hands in the
picture show.
I love shrimp and him,
and curling up
with his desert
sunset voice
painting with me
over the phone.

The Bush Dance

The Bush Dance

It's Lent on the rez. My cousins
gave up chocolate
in Jesus' name. They pretend to faint as I eat
their leftover Valentine stash.
So many taboos; not supposed to dance,
legs will turn to wood,
can't eat meat
on Friday, play the fiddle or cards.
A cousin tells of a recent *rugaroo* sighting.
The *rugaroo*, a black dog with red eyes, or a white stallion,
shape shifts into a man at night and has a habit
of hanging around the rez during Lent.
Changing back to beast before the sun's rays strike,
he risks a fiery explosion if he lingers too long.
He was seen dashing through the casino parking lot,
caught on the lone surveillance camera.

One night I walked backwards around my cousin's house
at midnight holding an Ace of Spades
to my forehead and met the devil.
I invited him to the bush dance.
Taw-pway, he said, *yes.* So we danced
the Red River Jig and Whiskey at Midnight,
got drunk on jugs of chokecherry wine,
jigged until our legs turned to wood,
and the *rugaroo* my cousin was dancing with
said *I gotta get the hell out of here before I burst into flames*
and the devil smiled. The priest came
and busted up the fiddle, so I went home
and played solitaire,
the Ace of Spades
in the devil's pocket.

Prairie Chicks

We teased the reservation Indian cousin,
us urban Indians knowing nothing about
the rez. Didn't even call it the rez yet,
like it used to be ghetto not the 'hood.'
Do you know what this is? A can opener!
Ha ha! *Aye, ho wah*! Can you dig it? Do ya
have TVs yet, plug them into the tipi pole?
Ayyeee. Oh, shoot, that was a goot one, yah,
goot, like the Navajos say, *Ya ta hey*! Got
some greasy goat meat, Hee hee. Yah, man,
she's a full blooded Sioux, raised with
the Chippewa. Yep, a dog eater with the
rabbit chokers! Shit ya, we just got here,
took the train in. Ya, we're prairie chicks,
from Turtle Mountains. Hey which one of
you said you'd like to turtle our mountains?
Hah, shit, you wish! No way, just cuz you're
from Browning. A drink? Shh, I don't want her
to hear. Like I brought her back here with me to
get away from the drinking. Ya, puts away a
goddamn six-pack to my one can! Fuckin' A, man,
ho, should see her fight. I wouldn't want to make
her mad. Hey, got some weed though?
Acapulco Gold, *ho wah*!
Far out, I can dig it man. Yah, this chick'll keep
on truckin', truckin' back to the prairie,
I'm takin' a trip to the Turtle Mountains.

Portland, 1970s

I walk barefoot on the hot cement,
downtown heat spews a rotten scent,
with hair long, eagle feather tied tight,
and bone chocker, fringed vest, bright
beads, hey cousin, spare a dime? Toss
it here. *Yellow jacket? Blue Cross?*
Sure. Buy a lid for ten bucks, super groovy,
and stoned watching Soldier Blue movie,
crying at the song by Buffy St. Marie,
a sense of pride, she's Cree like me.
Custer died in an arrow shirt, that's Indian Power;
Lizzie waits in the fort's phallus shaped tower.
The treaty said "as long as the grass
grows," and BIA means kiss my Big Indian Ass.
Wounded Knee '73, the taking of Alcatraz,
fishing rights, the Army engineers,
damned the mighty river, no salmon here
at Cooks Landing in Washington. The Coast
Guard rammed the elders' tiny fishing boats,
and BIA stands for Boss Indians Around.
Don't rock the boat, shut up, don't make a sound.
Honky go home! Go home and pack,
give us our land back, just give it back.
Hell no we won't go! Tricky Dicky,
make love not war, and I'm a hippy
living in a commune, stoned on free love
morning noon and night blowing smoke above
the barn where I'm high on sweet goat's breath
and leading anti-war marches, *no more death.*
Peace sign and flower power, a daisy for your gun,
tattered jeans, hiking boots, keep on truckin',
peace bro, peacefully pissed off and the body bag

count grows, commune men flee to Canada.
We march for women's liberation, black power
Dashiki's flow, Gay liberation, a pretty flower.
Hare Krishna, Hare Krishna, Krishna
Krishna, Hare Ramah, Hare Ramah

Ramah, Ramah. God is a crutch. Smoke a bowl?
groovy, far-out, can you dig it, can you roll
a joint? I'm getting low on my stash,
we're marching, marching to get our heads bashed.
Two white men, suits and ties, standing behind
me: *Barefoot and feathers, she must be an Indian.*

1969

Speed, uppers
Yellow Jackets
Blue Cross,
cleaning house
day after day for hours
tub not shiny enough
picking minute non-existing particles
off the rug incessantly
knife in hand with me to the bathroom
killer behind the door
daymares feed paranoia
someone behind the shower curtain
like in the Hitchcock movie
but I am skinny
so skinny
looking good in
tight mini skirt
counting the whistles
standing at the bus stop.

Shape Shifting Rugaroo

Grandpa Norman said once along the Red River
he and his friends saw a man turn into a horse.
They ran and took his clothes away.
Grandpa said when the sun rays
hit the *rugaroo* he exploded into flames.
Burned up.

Tracks

On Saturday afternoon my father dropped
Mom and I off at the beauty parlor
and headed for the bar.
I walked to the library
and entered the world of Narnia,
guided by the lantern light.

I carried an armload of books
back to the parlor in time to watch
Mom's tightly curled hair
become enveloped in a fog of Aqua Net.

We walked uptown to the bar,
I stopped at the door and watched
as she disappeared into the smoky room.

Soon my father brought a quarter
out and I skipped to the corner drug store,
ordered a chocolate milk shake,
took slow spins on the leather seat
after each sip, making it last
before I crawled into the car's back seat.

Toward sunset, orange
pop and potato chips arrived at the car door,
when he later staggered
out with pepperoni sticks
I knew I was in for a long night.

Their arguing woke me,
You worthless crippled whore bitch.
You're nothing but a damn dirty dog.

He drove wildly through the city streets.
You're millstones around my neck,
swinging the station wagon
onto the railroad tracks
as we screamed,
empty beer cans jigging crazily by my feet.
Through eight-year-old eyes the lantern light appeared
straight ahead blinking in and out of the fog,
the roar and whistle.

Father

1.

I'm eight years old kneeling by the tub
in the bathroom,
the only door that locks,
praying, hands folded,
left thumb over right,
a good Catholic girl,
Dear God burn down the bar
tonight before he leaves,
or plant a huge oak tree
in front of his car as he drives home.

But here you are: oily black
hair hanging over bleeding eyes
and loose lips, soon the sound
of *flux, flux* fists on skin, then boots.
I hide in the closet.

2.

Now you lay dying in the tribal nursing home
emaciated by Lucky Strikes and booze
all day at the Tomahawk Bar.

You moan, *my god, my god*
what did I do to deserve this?
I slam my knitting down
and want to scream
forty-two years
of your drunks, calling me
whore and slut when I was ten,
the twenty-eight stitches in mama's head,
then stop,

wondering should I feel guilty,
the man is dying.

    3.
Don't you come to my funeral
because, I'll sit up in my coffin
and spit in your face.
I kneel by your casket before the wake
begins, watching you,
frozen, cold, unmoving.

    4.
Crossing myself, I rise.

Home from Happy Rock

What do you want from me, blood?
Here, use this razor blade.
Go ahead and goddamn cut my wrists.
Get over here, quit running,
quit crying,
Where's your bitch sister?
I'll give you something to cry about,
watch me bleed to death
You want my blood?
What the hell do you want?
Goddammit,
bitches fuckin'
whores, where are you?
I'll cut my own wrist for you,
watch.
You can watch me bleed to death
then you'll be satisfied,
is that what you fucking want?
What do you want from me?
What more do you want from me?

Happy Pills

Great-grandma had a horse's face
and swung a mean *bagamaagan,*
the voyageurs hid the high wine from her,
no longer able to hunt buffalo
she probably needed Prozac.

Grandma would chase Grandpa
with a butcher knife, then retreat
to her room for days, refusing to eat.
The nuns beat her at boarding school
for speaking Cree.
She could have used Lithium.

The Stones wrote "Nineteenth Nervous
Breakdown" for my mother.
Relocation to the west coast was a shock.
My baby, bring me my happy pills.

I set the giant-sized bottle of aspirin
in front of me, and swallow two at a time.
In the bathroom mirror,
the eyes of my grandmothers stare back.

I lay in this white
room, nurses hush by,
red flowers startle the air,
my throat raw from tubes,
my heart beating out of control,
Post traumatic stress disorder.
Generational trauma.
Effexor, Zoloft, Zanax, Cymbalta.

Bring me my happy pills.

Hopeless Was the Ticker Tape

Hopeless was the ticker
                word that scudded
                        across my brain today,
the front lobe,
          destined
                for a lobotomy,
Like the churlish
          Indian in *One Flew*
                Over the Cuckoo's Nest
taking pills two at a time,
          two at a time,
                        losing count
I am the Indian surrounded
          by the fog, a shroud,
                a phantasm,
                        disappearing.

Foster Father

And the foster father had two Cadillacs
And the foster father had a house beautiful,
And the foster father drank Seven Highs on the rocks,
And the foster father had a new wife, a saucy redhead.
And the foster father took the foster girl to his empty rental house.

And the foster father grabbed her from behind
and clutched at her breasts,

and I said,
I'll kill you if you do that again,
and I'll tell the redhead.

Mother Superior

Rising as she entered class
a quiet shussing rustle
Good morning, mother superior
thirty voices in unison,
her huge draping rosary,
black habit's ominous
cavernous sleeves
to put her hands in.

I was called back to the cloak closet
with its rank smell of wet wool coats,
unbuckled black galoshes,
neatly lined along,
the heavy paneled wall,
the waxed wooden floors,
puddles under umbrellas

Say the Act of Contrition
my child
her ruler slid out of the sleeve, poised.
I stumbling,
—*and I detest all my sins . . . um . . .*
the pains of hell—

Hands held out
trembling in the
cloak closet.

St. Peter, 1957

I walk to Safeway helping Sister Genevieve
carry groceries back to the convent,
my braids as blue black as her habit, swishing
back and forth, her rosary beads clicking
like the genuflector cricket during high mass.
I can't speak, she keeps the silence, peering
down at me to keep me in place.
My homemade wool flannel jumper is itchy,
my muslin blouse bleached a ghostly white.

I stay after school,
avoiding the Italian kids calling me squaw,
hurling rocks like bullets.
I receive a scapular from Sister,
and wrap it around my neck
with the others, tucked away under
my ghost shirt.

Oz

I cross myself with Holy Water
and melt like the wicked witch of
the west. I'm dying laying
in a puddle beneath
the Glenda gaze
of St.
Ann

Patent Leather Shoes

My first pair
of black patent leather shoes

took them shiny from the box
eagerly put them on
brushed silver hair from my face
smoothed my skirt
and stared down

couldn't see the reflection
of my bloomers

in the darkness
in the lovely darkness

the nuns lied
the boys would not have seen my underwear
if I'd been allowed to wear patent leather shoes
at confirmation.

Denver March

For Grace Gillette

Surprising to see so many dancers'
outfits sewn with dragonfly material,
men's traditional shirts,
jingle dresses, shawls,
Gracie Her Many Horses' floaty fancy dance dress.
Then there was my friend,
her bedroom dressed to the max in dragonflies,
sheets, pillowcases,
gauzy scarves, hand sewn jackets,
material with painted and jeweled wings,
huge faceted brooches,
heavy turquoise necklaces,
wrap around eyes,
brilliant blues, vermillion, pearl.

After a car accident, she had sat in her backyard,
bruised and shaken.
Dragonflies gathered and flew all around me.
She called her brother up north, searching for meaning.
Didn't your parents teach you anything?
They are our ancestors healing you.

My dancing friends,
knowing something I didn't,
their awareness, acute vision.
I wasn't paying attention,
until Red Lake.

The Eagles Dance

The Eagles Dance

For Loretta DeLong

When I was laying with my face
on the ground,
two eagles came and picked me up,
Kinew Ikwe and Miigizi.
They carried me to the Turtle Mountain
Niimiwin. I watched the eagles dance;
then White Wolf invited me to join the circle.
I danced with Buffalo,
shoulders bowed, graceful.
I danced with Bear, back and forth,
to rasping songs,
then two stepped with Rabbit.
I round danced with Skunk and Porcupine.
Look to the South, where Healing is found.
Look to the North, towards Wisdom.
The Anishinaabe gathered told me,
find who you are, find morning star.
The eagles said, *you are morning star,*
your name is Morning Star
Grandma Greatwalker danced
by with two elders wearing jingle dresses,
turning they swept their arms forward
and said, *these healing dresses are yours,*
then Sun, wrapped in his scarlet robe, danced west,
as Nookomis danced me home.

Tonight the Train

For Mark Turcotte

1.

Tonight the goddamned 7th cavalry charged through,
bugles blaring;

frets through town, a feverish child;

heralded its entrance with trumpets, bells
a king returning from battle;

shrieked, licentious in orgasmic coupling.

Tonight the train's a woman's distressed plea;

carried a buoy, a passing barge on the prairie.

Tonight is Veteran's Day, blessed silence.
Let the warriors sleep.

2.

Tonight a tornado approached from the west,
        sirens screaming, I sprang into my shelter.

Tonight was spring's first thunder;
        I carried my pipe outside for its blessing.

Tonight I heard the rumbling of hooves, felt the earth shake
        and sat on top of the Pembina Hills watching the buffalo
        go by for a day and a night and a day, bellowing.

But it was only the train.

Grand Forks

Some nights the traffic
on 42nd Street keeps me awake,

a whine-induced insomnia.
Even the dresser-top water

fountain is pissed, irritated
I didn't understand what it was saying

the other night. And now the goddamned train,
how can anyone *live* here?

I want to wake up in the Turtle Mountains
listening to susurrus of aspen leaves,

the echo of loons across the lake,
the quiet of beaver trafficking

heavy loads though watery highways.
I long for the sound of *sibising,*

drumming over rocks,
speaking to me in Chippewa.

Sweet Water Well

The paved road abruptly ends and we roll in a choking cloud of dust into Cannonball. My sticky mouth coated and dry. Grandpa waves to us from his tarpaper shack.

We'd driven from Oregon to Cannonball, North Dakota, that summer I was eleven. The stifling heat made bearable only by frequent stops for orange pop. I cheered at the sign *Entering the Standing Rock Sioux Reservation.*

Tonhse keya and *paypithtikway, shahmock*! He shouts in Cree.

Strange how no one questioned these Crees living with the Sioux. Caught in a winter blizzard on their way north and offered the church sanctuary, they never left. It helped that Great-grandma was a medicine woman. Hearing of the sick she gathered herbs, roots, leaves, and bark from the rich river bottom land. Put in a glass of water, if the medicine moved in a circle it was right for you.

I run to the well, toss off the cover, pull the rope hand over hand and slurp the cool sweet water from the *mekwon* until my stomach is full to burst, and water spurts from my nose.

As Great-grandma fired up the wood stove to make coffee I snuck down to the Missouri river until I heard my dad yelling and caught hell because of rattlesnakes.

In the hissing of the kerosene lamp I lay down on the blanketed wood floor drinking in the sweet flow of Cree.

Holy Hamm's Beer

The Fargo Bishop intoned that this will be
a special Indian Mass *for all of thee.*
We gathered on the hill. The mission church
enthroned above the town enjoyed its perch.
The nuns played the "Indian" drums;
they look to me like bongos from
Jamaica. The mass is held in honor
of a tribal member prostrate on the floor
becoming an Indian Deacon. He seeks our prayer
through song and ceremony gathered there.
The drums reverberate in earnest now
across the ruck and ruin of the reservation,
the drum is heard in noisy expostulation.
The nuns begin to sing triumphantly
Holy, Holy, Holy, Ho-oh-ly!
I believe they sing to all of us Catechumen
in my father's favorite sappy drinking tune,

From the Land of Sky Blue Wa-ah-ter—
Comes the beer refreshing, Hamms, the beer refreshing!

The happy bear in Indian dress careens
on black-and-white television screens
dancing to the bongo drum and so
my father dances out the room to go
to the kitchen, to the fridge that's near
to get himself a can of Indian beer,
which he opens with the church key
and offers a solemn toast *to all of thee.*

Drunkard's Mass

St. Ann invites her pious flock,
Sitting in reverent, silent prayer,
To Saturday mass at five o'clock;
It's early evening, you are there,
Sorry for a week of sinning,
Always trying to do what's right,
At our casino caught embezzling,
But Celebrant you've seen the light!
Your sins descend the church's aisle
With ten Our Fathers, five Hail Marys;
No fear of Purgatory cramps your style;
Your Saturday habit never varies,
Listening to the homilies,
Drinking wine to ease your ache,
And now Communion on your knees.
Shaking Father's hands you shake
And jig your way out to your car;
A dashboard Jesus points the way,
A mile of gravel, to Betty's Bar,
A sanctuary where you stay,
Ambrosia flowing from its chalice,
Drinking deep, you park your ass,
In the forgiveness present in Betty's palace,
Courtesy of the drunkard's mass;
Tonight you'll put your soul in hock,
Let it pour or rain sunshine,
Because next week at five o'clock
You'll be forgiven one more time.

May 11, 1980

My six-year-old daughter
tells me when she grows
up she's going to be White.

As I flip through a magazine,
she sees a picture of a White
lady in a bathing suit,
see, I want to be big and white
like her. Um, brown is okay,
she says, sweeping her tiny hand
at her brown legs,
but I want to be White
when I get big.

In the tub playing with Barbie dolls,
she shakes the blonde, pale skinned one,
you're beautiful.
She shakes the brown one,
a gift from me,
and you're ugly.

Coming out of the bath,
her face a rose brown,
her eyes questioning, anxious,
mom, is my face
just a little white?

Uncle Gus and Aunt Veronica

Norwegian he, and French and Cree was she
Of Turtle Mountain hills and lakes, you see,
He off the boat from Norway, as you construe—
The land of fiords and solid mountains light blue.
So they married, seemingly contraire;
She in braids dark black, he with a blonder hair.
Oh yes, two different tongues they spoke in life
Which often caused them strife.
"Dese" and *"dems"* and *"dose,"* you would hear.
Or, *"yah,"* and "tank you *wh'ery* much, my dear."
On canning day she sent for vinegar.
"Yah, I'll go and get you *whiniger."*
"Vinegar! dhat's how I say it, me!
One more *uff-dah* and you will drive me crazy!"
He turned to her with a smile and a tease,
"You don't get mad when *ere* you hear me say,
'*Where-ron-i-ca*—come *o'r* here, please, I say.'"

North Dakota

I'm from Nor' Dakota, me
From da reservation up 'dere,
We surrounded by Swedes
Dey fight da Norwegian's, I swear.
Dey live close by us because
Da mighty Pembina Band
With Gatling guns aimed,
Signed a treaty, and lost ten million acres of land
And hills, and sweeping prairie,
In 'dis here place you call Nor' Dakota.
As long as the grass grows
And the river flows . . .
And now I lie upon the earth in bitter cold,
Close to the Red River's frozen edge,
And under layers of snow no longer ours,
I hear the grass grow.

North Dakota on a Sunny Thirty below Zero Day

Kookum, with smiling eyes,
says to my daughter gazing
in awe at the rainbow sun dogs,
crystalline and brilliant against the cobalt sky,
It's so cold, even the sun
has ear muffs on!

La Quette

The Head Start bus
honks for the neighbors' child,
and I see you wave
your chubby fist at me.

Your long black hair braided
so tight, you hold the corners of your eyes,
your stomach full of bannock dipped in bacon grease.

I lay
back down and curl
up into myself,
like the folded fall leaves
scraping outside.

Kicking Thunder

For Sky Boy

You screamed in terror
at the storm low overhead.
The thunder stunned
and shook the stucco cottage,
an old tribal house,
but you found no comfort
in my arms.
Fleeing to your room,
coming out wearing only
a pamper and new cowboy boots,
you marched right past me
heading for the door as the hail
tore through the white electric air.
Alarmed, I cried out
Where are you going, son?
Calm resolve now, a soldier to battle.
I'm going out to kick the thunder!
and marched forward until I swept
you up and held your brave
heart close to mine.

Answers

A young, light skinned hand
urgently waving.

"Are you really an Indian?"

"Yes, I am Chippewa, my great grandmothers
were medicine women; grandmother
smoked *kinnikinnik* in a corn cob pipe;
I know the smell of smoked moose hide, of
sage and sweet grass;
Yes! I am Indian."

"Where are your feathers?"

"My Eagle feathers, bearer of messages to Manitou,
stroked gently in prayer,
are lovingly packed away;
my Eagle wing dances with me
and is held high on the
drum's honor beats."

"How!" a bold blue eyed boy shouts.

My ears hear the *hau kola* of the Lakota,
a happy greeting. The *hau*! Of an elder
listening intently.
Through the darkness of a sacred
ceremony, I hear *hau*! At prayers end,
when all is well.

"Do you still live in tipis?"

"No, my little friend, but I miss
  sleeping next to Mother Earth,
  in the Circle of her Womb,
  gazing at stars, blurred by sleep and smoke."

"I saw a drunken Injun!"

Laughter. Give me strength.
Help them to understand.

"Yes, my people are in pain.
  the wine fog hides cement cities
  and clears to vast prairies,
  proud warriors, racing free, strong,
  bodies moving one with their horses'
  where once again the
  Eagle's cry is heard."

Crazy Horse

They say a medicine pouch
that belonged to Crazy Horse
has dragonflies on each corner,
and his shield,
housed in the Smithsonian,
has dragonflies and lightening symbols.

Calling his ancestors
to be with him in battle,
strength,
acute vision
a whirlwind,
elusive maneuvers
swift in victory,
healing,
his protector,
this holy creature.

Round Dance
by Red Lake

Round Dance by Red Lake

The announcer invited the audience
    and all dancers to step into the arena,
        everybody up, join in, grab a snag,

aye, you can't get jealous.
    The arena filled with ribbon shirts, cowboy boots
        moccasins, Pendleton coats,

women draped in shawls,
    dance in a circle
        a sunwise circle

a healing friendship dance,
    hold hands and sway
        linked to this world

and others beyond;
    I saw Makwa dancing with us,
        heard Mahiingan howling,

Kinew's head bobbing,
    bells ringing, dew claws
        clicking in soft rhythm to

brother deer's drum.
    Nookomis leads the way
        along with nearby planets,

Milky Way stars dance
    to the heartbeat of Aki.
        In the cool lake air I breathe

her visible breath
    I am Aki's daughter,
        indinawemaagan

Starvation Winter, 1888

My grandmother slices
her wrist
and presses it
to the wailing
mouth of her infant.

Sisters of War, Lacrosse

On the great English King's birthday
the Chippewa said to the commandant
we will play baaga'adowe
by the fort's gates for your amusement.

The Michilimackinac Jesuit priest
forbid all Mide ceremonies,
but he approved the game played
with a stick resembling his bishop's crosier.

That night, *ikwewag miimiwag*, the women danced
wrapped in calico, waving handkerchiefs,
tongues rattling, they encouraged their men.

Lord Amherst wrote: Could it be contrived
to send smallpox among the tribes?
We gave them two blankets
and a handkerchief
out of the smallpox hospital.
I hope it will have the desired effect.

The *ogimah inini* announced
tomorrow we play the Creator's game!
He prayed with his *opwaagan*,
willow bark smoke circled the camp.

That night six hundred Chippewa and Sauk
danced for healing, for strength,
and fearlessness, to be quick as foxes—
no brittle rabbit legs here.

The cannon discharged that sultry morning,
and the face-off began. The soldiers watched,
drinking tea, enjoying the frenzied scene,
the players faces and bodies painted in ceremonial colors.

A sudden overhand, the leather ball shot
as if by accident into the fort's garrison.
The teams rushed the gate.

Ogichida ikwewag, sisters of war, handed them guns,
knives, and *bagamaagan* hidden
in their dresses and shawls,
and drew them from Lord Amherst's blankets.
That night they wrapped
their blankets tight
joining the victory dance
waving handkerchiefs high,
sisters of war, le le lee!

Circles

Walking with my grandchildren
across the narrow coastal road,
winds that have permanently bent cliff trees low
now succumb to the forest of cedar trees
whose mossy veils absorbed
the ocean's breath,
a sudden hush as though entering a church
or earth lodge.
These children
earlier dancing on the beach and shouting at ocean waves
now feel compelled to whisper
along the pine needle path,
touching grandmother cedar trees,
their bark gray, streaked from rain.
Now a game of holding each other up, heads bent
far back trying to see the top.
Scattered around the forest floor lay what tribal elders
call nurse logs, with sharp and perfect young trees,
growing straight, their roots cinctured
to the fallen titans, taking solid purchase,
young, taking sustenance from her,
bringing her back to life.
Children, our living breath.

Kookum

Kookum picked *kinnikinnik*
for me before the first thunder.
Sitting on a hill under the old burr oak tree,
with knives in hand peeling off the outer
blood red bark curling the inner.
The priest stopped by with two nuns in tow.
What are you doing
Josephine, making wiener sticks?
You slapped your hand over your mouth
shaking in silent laughter
and almost rolled down the hill,
then went with the rest inside
to receive communion.
Mine continued out below the oak.

Sun Dogs

Are winter's parentheses
To the sun's cool comment.

Winter's Night

I saw Death standing by my bedroom
door in the thick of a winter's night.

Silent, he stood there arms at his side.
He wore a long gray robe;
I felt him gazing at me.
I searched to see his face
in the hooded shadow.
I flung the covers away and sat up to go with him,
but he turned and left without me so I laid back down.

I wake in the black of night,
and, sometimes sorrowfully,
realize I am still alive.
I keep the bedroom door open.

The Rain Was Warm and Mild

and drifted over camp,
the dancing had to stop,
our moccasins were damp
their soles starting to sop.
The caller had a thought
of having shirtless men
(Not that he'd get caught!)
go sliding on the ground
through a pool of water
on bellies large and round.
We shouted yes in laughter,
a man began to beam
and, stepping to the gate,
he peeled his shirt (the screams!)
and in a moment's wait
went flying for a ride,
the parted waves shot out
in sheets on either side,
his eyes were tightly shut
his braids went straight behind.
He flew with all his might
his shorts were in a bind,
his lips were pursed and tight.
Our aching sides were sore
from laughing at the clown,
he entered Indian lore,
he'd never live it down,
a legend among all men.
The story'd be told for years,
we'd laugh some more again
and wipe away our tears.
The young began to sing

with sadness in their voice
and all around the ring
we listened to their choice,
in double beat they sang
the song of a mother's heart,
across the camp it rang,
a wisdom they'd impart
that only youth can see,
their voices clear and high
in familiar melody,
made the elders cry.
Don't forget your past,
Listen to your elders,
Culture's going fast.
Hey-ya hey-ya hey.
Now dancing to the beat
as spirits guide our way
with buffalo calls we meet
the challenge of each day
we have to take a stance
we're facing all our fears,
we dance, we dance, we dance
to wipe away the tears.

Tribal Council Candidate

Please note: Tribal council candidate question and answer panel is scheduled for October 6th, Wednesday 1:00 at the Sprung Structure Bingo Hall.

● ● ●

Please note: Panel scheduled for October 6th has been cancelled due to lack of interest.

● ● ●

Tonshe! My name is Joe *"Che Boy"* Moliere, and I'm a District I candidate for tribal council. My father is Manard *"Che Man"* Moliere, and my mom is Cherrie *"Che Fe"* (nee LaPlante) Moliere. My grandfather was the late Larry *"LaPuhsh"* Moliere, and my grandmother is Jenny *"LaJang"* Moliere-LaPierre. I was born and raised on the reservation and I'm a card carrying ½ Michif, me.

I picked rocks, raspberries at a farm, and dumped potatoes in the valley, did surveying for the Bureau, and made ladders in a factory. As youse can see I've had leadership responsibilities and experiences most of my life, and it has prepared me to lead the tribe in the right direction.

I'm a tribal member in good standing, never got no floater off the rez. I am proud to say I had my embezzling record expunged by the tribal court. I am an experienced choice for a strong stable government; your vote is the voice for a new start, together let's begin a new future.

I represent honesty, dependability, and respect for our people. My main concern is jobs, jobs, jobs. For a new future with new ideas like jobs, jobs, and more jobs, vote for me! I will lead our tribe into the future. I believe our current leaders have lost the concept of TRIBE and are simply a bunch of individuals! While respecting the past, I will address the needs of today with honesty, integrity, unity through diversity, and job creation strategy!

I support the culture. Let's learn from our Elders by treating each other with respect and dignity. I stand for the elders. I don't brag about myself, that's not tradish, but you people may recall that I was the "Chief" mascot at the girls' state basketball championship game.

I will use common sense, and the advice of the people. If elected I will build an 18 hole golf course, YMCA, a Wal-Mart, and a nursing home with swing beds and basic beds too.

I listen to the people with competence, vision, and commitment. Let's move forward with Energy! Enthusiasm! Excellence! Youse all know our tribe has been in dire straits, so let's stabilize our tribe—we have our ups and downs, doesn't mean we have to fall apart. With the turmoil in the Middle East, we could very well be next in getting bombed, so if youse are looking for good honest leadership and someone that is really concerned, vote for me.

To boot, according to the U.S. Census more than half our tribal members are women, ho wah! Yet, in the last 20 years, less than 3% of our tribal government has been represented by women, whah whah! Your vote for me is a vote for equality, for change, for progress, civil rights, for treaty rights, employment rights; I will make it tribal policy! I stand behind fair hiring (but I ask youse, do we really want another woman chairman?).

Your concerns are my concerns. I listen to the people. I will represent the underrepresented. I've returned your calls. I apologize to those I have not been able to visit; I work long hours, from sunrise to sunset.

Elections Day is coming—a day marked in history, remember, I can only help youse if youse help me, this is true sovereignty at work. Hope is on the way! I'll be voting for myself, I'm an equal opportunity leader. If youse need a ride, call me at my ma's house over 'dere on Piss Road—I'll come pick youse up in my van to go vote at the K.C. Hall, (treats and refreshments will be served in the van, if youse know what I mean).

Vote for your future! Your vote is your voice for a new start. I want your vote! Check number three on the ballot for District One. Your vote is greatly appreciated.

Tank youse for allowing me 'dis opportunity to help youse become more familiar wit me.

Che Boy

P.S. The end of this TERROR is coming in two weeks!

(Paid for by the Elect Che Boy Committee, Archie LaBunkum, President)

Waabishi-ma'iingan

I had just killed two school board
members, drove them off a cliff.
I survived the fall and climbed
on top of the underbelly of the van
and was doing a victory dance
when you appeared,
the frozen air turning to black,
accenting your mantle of snow.
I froze waiting for your attack.
In a sudden fit of fury
I stomped and raged in the crystal air,
determined not to be easy prey;
I will be the maker of my death, not you.
Gazing expressionless, we stare
into each other's eyes.
You turn and walk into the sacred night.

Anishinaabe before Columbus

Anishinaabe before Columbus;
driving elk, freely
going hunting in junipers.
Kind language, Midewiwin. Nations! Ojibwe;
Porcupine quills, regular
stitches, tiny upon velvet.

Wearisome xenophobic Yankee Zealots.

Turtle Mountain Orchid

Alongside the walking trail by Fish Lake
an orchid grows in the Turtle Mountains.
Small pale blossoms, hardly significant
she stands modestly among the rich rot smell of leaves.

Spotted Coral Root found in the forested
areas where they are parasitic or saprophytic
on underground plant roots or debris.

Elders tell of the Chippewa
buried along the banks of the lake
during the smallpox epidemic,
so many died, whole families
with no one left to bury them;
log homes were burned with bodies inside.

We used the dried stems of the orchid
to create a tea for pneumonia victims,
but it was useless against this new disease.

·Lacking chlorophyll, they get their food
directly from dead organic matter.

I back away slowly reverently
afraid to touch its fragile beauty,
leaving it to draw life from
the decay of other beings,
transforming the past into the future.

GLOSSARY

Aki: Mother Earth
baaga'adowe: lacrosse
bagamaagan: war club
ikwewag miimiwag: the women dance
ishkoonigan: leftover land
kinnikinnik: tobacco made from inner bark of Red Willow
kookoosh: boogeyman
Kookum: Grandmother
Manitou: Creator
mekwon: ladle
Mide: Midewiwin
Nookomis: Grandmother
obodashkwanishi: dragonfly
ogichida ikwewag: warrior women
ogimah inini: male leader
opwaagun: pipe
Paypithtikway: Come in!
rugaroo: a bad spirit that shape shifts from a black dog to a man during Lent
Shahmock: Right now!
sibising: Little Stream that Sings
taw-pway: agreement; yes
Tonshe keya: How are you?
Waabishi-ma'iingan: White Wolf
ziibaaska'iganagooday: jingle dress

Previously Published

Drunken Boat
"Bag Balm"
"The Reservation Dump"
"Starvation Winter" ("Starvation Winter, 1888")
"To My Sister"

Florida Review
"The Bush Dance"
"Father"

North Country
"Indian Angel in 1st Grade"
"The Rain Was Warm and Mild"

Sporting Words
"Bagataway, Little Sister of War" (Sisters of War, Lacrosse")

Story Telling Time
"The Eagles Dance"
"Midnight in North Dakota"
"The Moccasin Trail"

Yellow Medicine Review
"My Grandfather Was a New Initiate"
"Ogichida Ikwe" ("*Ogichida Ikwewag*")
"The Quilt"
"Turtle Mountain Orchid"